DALE PARTRIDGE

Edited by the Relearn.org Theological Advisory Board

house church

The Doctrines, Convictions, & Liturgy
of a Biblical House Church

Aiden Watson

BEND, OREGON

A living document.

DEDICATION

To the church planters—those who see the Kingdom and, who by God's grace, further its borders through sacrifice, labor, and love. May God bless you and guide you in your ministry.

This is not a book

In your hands is a document—a written resource for house church goers and house church planters. For that reason, do not expect this composition to read like a book. In fact, consider it to be more like a comprehensive "about" section on a local church's website. Because house churches do not generally have websites, those within the Relearn.org House Church Network host their Statement of Faith, doctrines, convictions, and order of worship in this printed publication.

What is Relearn.org?

Relearn.org is a global house church planting ministry focused on training, establishing, and supporting small biblical communities. Relearn.org is not a theological denomination but rather an association of house churches operating within the historic evangelical church, confessions, and creeds. To learn more about us visit Relearn.org.

For those interested in planting or pastoring a biblical house church, consider enrolling in our one-year, seminary-grade, *Diploma of Ecclesiology* program at our companion ministry, StJustins.org.

Published in Bend, Oregon, by Aiden Watson, LLC.
Written by Dale Partridge
Cover Design by Dale Partridge

For information, please contact us through our website at Relearn.org.

Table of Contents

Statements

Doctrines

Convictions

Free-Worship Liturgy

Section One

WELCOME

• *Gratissimum* •

Fruitfulness Flows from Structure

*"I have chosen the way of faithfulness;
I set your rules before me."*

PSALM 119:30

There is no one perfect way to conduct the local church meeting. That is, our ministry is not claiming ultimate knowledge or flawless interpretation of the Bible on these matters. But we do have a considerable amount of Scripture available to us for creating biblically accurate Christian gatherings. While many of these ecclesiological doctrines have been buried, forgotten, or carefully cut out of the modern church practice, we feel that unearthing of God's original architecture is essential.

Furthermore, we believe church fruitfulness flows largely from structure. In fact, we believe spiritual fruitfulness can be greatly promoted or prevented by structure alone. This principle is demonstrated all around us. For example, biblically structured marriages principally generate spiritually healthy homes. Biblically structured homes generally produce spiritually healthy children. Because we believe that God's Word does not return void (Is. 55:11), we believe those who earnestly seek God's design for the local church will find that it too, will yield spiritually healthy sheep.

Now structure without the Spirit will leave us only with a moral association of infertile people—a gathering of individuals polished in formation but bankrupt in spiritual power. Like all things of the Christian life, "Unless the Lord builds the house, they labor in vain who build it" (Ps. 127:1). That is to say, we are not looking to activate orderly churches who hold a form of godliness without the power. No. We are looking to help devout, regenerated Christians who are dedicated to the building of God's Kingdom, in God's timing, according to God's Word.

As you have likely noticed by the cover of this publication, the content of this document is focused on building biblical churches within houses and not buildings. Nevertheless, we do not believe that biblical church is limited to the house. In truth, we believe there are many biblical churches that gather in buildings, public school auditoriums, community centers, and even under trees. It is merely our conviction that houses offer a uniquely intimate, sustainable, universal, and fruitful expression of church that is harder to accomplish in a larger group setting. That said, and to be very clear, we are arm-in-arm with our Christian brothers who are shepherding traditional churches around the world. We hold the same biblical ecclesiology; we're just carrying it out in a different format. It is our sincere hope that if the Lord is calling you to join or plant a biblical house church, whether domestic or international, whether civilly free or greatly persecuted, that this document and its humble perspective becomes a useful tool for your journey.

Welcome

Getting Clear

*"But grow in the grace and knowledge of our
Lord and Savior Jesus Christ."*

2ND PETER 3:18

The longer you follow Christ, the more you will understand
His nature. However, this is easier said than done. Our
modern culture has created so many different caricatures
of Jesus that many have lost the biblical Jesus altogether.
Nonetheless, after an honest reading of the Gospels, you
quickly learn one truth central to His ministry—He wasn't
interested in winning people under false expectations. In
fact, Jesus went out of His way to make sure people had
a very clear view of what it meant to follow Him. He
demonstrates this principle in Luke 14:25-30; 33 (NKJV)
when He says:

"Now great multitudes went with Him. And He turned
and said to them, "If anyone comes to Me and does not
hate his father and mother, wife and children, brothers and

21

sisters, yes, and his own life also, he cannot be My disciple. And whoever does not bear his cross and come after Me cannot be My disciple. For which of you, intending to build a tower, does not sit down first and count the cost, whether he has enough to finish it—lest, after he has laid the foundation, and is not able to finish, all who see it begin to mock him, saying, 'This man began to build and was not able to finish'?... So likewise, whoever of you does not forsake all that he has cannot be My disciple."

Jesus was unambiguous about what He expected of His followers. He didn't sugarcoat the level of commitment or cost involved in following Him, either. Instead, He was upfront and direct. What a contrast from many of today's churches who are focused more on comforting people than they are at communicating to them the Bible's expectations for those who follow Christ.

Like Jesus, this booklet is intended to be upfront and direct—to make it clear what it means to join a biblical church—that is—a church who is deeply committed to adhering to the Bible's model for Christian assembly. We believe God is clear and purposeful when it comes to the design and infrastructure of the local church. In fact, the intricate and elaborate instructions for the Old Testament Tabernacle and Temple are explicit evidence of this truth. God is a God of order and He is not silent about His expectations for His people. It is from this place that we must begin—a place which starts not with a goal for size, popularity, or success but with a heart for scriptural accuracy and fruitfulness.

Allow me to clarify with a brief illustration... There's an old phrase that reigns true in the church arena—what you win people with is what you win people to. That is to say, if a church wins folks with coffee shops, light-hearted messages, and childcare, then they have won those individuals to those things. However, the Scriptures call local churches to win people to three specific things—the Gospel, the Bible, and the covenant people of God.

That is the goal of this document. There is no striving to win your attendance at any particular church by any special offer or attraction. There is no hope to earn your commitment through a hidden agenda or unclear expectations. To be frank, it is quite the opposite. This document will outline everything from our church network's formal Statement of Faith to our interpretation of Scripture on giving, gender roles, and church governance.

Ultimately, this document is both a declaration and an introduction to the doctrines, convictions, and liturgy of a biblical house church. As you will learn through your review, we are a church network who loves Christ and His Word. We are a church network which believes in the authority of Scripture. But most of all, we are a church network that hopes to be found faithful by the Lord. However, any church you are considering will not be a perfect church, but if it is a church that allows the Scriptures to guide its gathering, then exercise your patience as you make your evaluation.

In a world filled with churches who seem spiritually

lethargic and lost, it is our sincere hope to offer you the information required to help you and your family determine if a biblical house church is right for you.

May the Lord lead you in this journey.

Overview

Why Church Membership?

*"But now God has set the members, each one
of them, in the body just as He pleased."*

1ST CORINTHIANS 12:18

For many, "church membership" can feel like a dirty word. However, this shouldn't surprise us in our individualistic and freedom-focused culture. As you might know, it is not uncommon to find nomad Christians who move from church to church, always avoiding a formal commitment to a body of believers. Even more, these hide-and-seek Christians find themselves dangerously independent, never submitting themselves to the care of elders and never experiencing the beauty of accountable, Christian community.

I want to initiate this discussion with a question: As a Christian, do you believe that God calls you to help build a healthy local church? To put that differently, do you think God expects you not only to consume but to contribute to the strengthening of your local church? I believe He does.

However, in order for you to invest in a local church, you must first become a committed and participating member of that assembly of believers. But what does that really mean?

Becoming a church member is just another way of saying you have formally committed yourself to a local assembly of Christians who operate as a church according to Scripture. This assembly would include regular and consistent gatherings (Acts; 2:40-47; Acts 20:7; 1 Cor. 16:1-2) where believers can receive the teaching of God's Word (1 Tim. 4:13; 2 Tim. 4:2), can serve and edify one another through the proper use of spiritual gifts (Rom. 12:3-8; 1 Cor. 12:4-31; 1 Pet. 4:10-11), engage in biblically ordered Sunday meetings (1 Cor. 14:26-40; 1 Tim 2-3), submit to the care and authority of biblically qualified elders (Heb. 13:7; Heb. 13:17; 1 Thes. 5:12-13; 1 Tim. 5:17-20), participate in the ordinances of baptism and communion (Luke 22:19; Acts 2:38-42), and proclaim the Gospel to those who don't believe (Matt. 28:18-20).

With this understanding, to attend a local church and refuse to formalize your membership with that body of believers demonstrates an unawareness of what it truly means to be a member of the Body of Christ. But the consequences of this refusal don't end at mere ignorance. This desire for autonomy also detaches us from the many blessings that come from such a commitment. Sadly, in a church culture that gives these benefits freely to anyone who shows up on Sunday, we must be reminded that these spiritual advantages are explicitly reserved for baptized, committed, submitted, and united members of a local church. I have listed them below for your review:

The Blessings of Local Church Membership

1. Daily and weekly fellowship.
(Col. 3:16; Acts 2:42–47, Acts 20:7; Heb. 10:24–25)

2. Spiritual warnings and encouragement.
(1 Thes. 5:11; Heb. 10:23–25)

3. Accountability to Scripture.
(Gal. 6:1–5; Col. 3:16; Jam. 5:16; 20; Luke. 17:3)

4. Communion with the saints.
(John 6:53–58; 1 Cor. 10:16; 1 Cor. 11:25–26; Acts 2:42)

5. Use and development of spiritual gifts.
(1 Cor. 12:4–11; Eph. 4:11–16; Rom. 1:11; Rom. 12:3–8)

6. Protection from doctrinal heresy.
(Acts 20:28–29; 2 Tim 4:2; Tit. 1:9; Tit. 1:10–11; 1 John 4:1)

7. Guidance toward godly living.
(Eph. 4:15; 25; 29 1 John 3:18; 1 Pet. 1:22; Heb. 10:23–25)

8. Spiritual ministering to the family.
(1 Thes. 5:11; Eph. 4:12; 29; 1 Cor. 14:26; Jude 1:20)

9. Giving in support of the Christian ministry.

(Rom. 12:13; Gal. 6:2; Heb. 13:16; Prov. 3:27-28)

10. Support in spiritual, emotional, physical or financial need.

(Rom. 12:10; Gal. 5:13; Col. 3:16; Jam. 5:16)

11. Discipline in times of sin.

(Gal. 6:1; Tit. 3:10-11; Jam. 5:19-20; Luke 17:3-4; 2 Thes. 3:14-15)

12. Equipping for personal ministry.

(Ephesians 4:11-12; Titus 2:1-5;; 1 Peter 4:11; 1 Pet. 4:10)

Understanding the Biblical Church

Jesus Christ has one Church seen in two expressions—local and universal. The first includes professing believers in Jesus Christ, who assemble in a congregation at a particular location on a regular basis, and the second includes all professing believers in Jesus Christ (past, present, and future) living across the globe.

As you likely know, the New Testament often uses metaphoric language when describing the local church. For example, we see it represented as a body, a family, a building, a bride, a house, and a flock (Rom. 12:4-5; Rev. 21:9; 2 Cor. 6:18; Heb. 3:6; Acts 20:28). In these metaphors, it's made clear that we are not random, individual parts but a collected and identified group. In reference to the church as a flock, the Bible does not imply we are a mixed bunch of goats, sheep, pigs, lambs, and rams—we are a pure and unified flock of one identity. The shepherds of the flock know which sheep are under their care and protection, and the sheep are certain who is guiding, feeding, and protecting their welfare (Acts 20:28; 1 Peter 5:1-4).

While these church-appointed shepherds are by no means the Chief Shepherd, I once heard a seasoned pastor say, "Those called to local pastoral ministry have the rich wisdom of Psalm 23 and John 10:1-30 to which they can learn the ways, desires, and direction of their Lord." It is in these passages which reveal the deeply committed relationship between the sheep and their shepherd. "My sheep hear My voice, and I know them, and they follow Me" (John 10:27). Charles Spurgeon once said in relationship to this truth, "When a local church functions under a biblical order if one sheep strays from the flock their absence will not go unnoticed—the shepherd(s) of that congregation will take note and labor to restore the sheep with great hope (Matthew 18:12-13)."

As mentioned above, the church is also seen as a building where each Christian is a living stone—each stone has a definite place and is not disjointed or in part-time use (1 Pet. 2:5). Charles Spurgeon beautifully affirms this metaphor, too, when he said, "Christian, you are a brick. What is the brick made for? It's made to build a house." The Apostle Paul also upholds this imagery when he tells us that the Church is "Built on the foundation of the apostles and prophets, Christ Jesus himself being the cornerstone..." (Eph. 2:20). Essentially, we are God's building—His temple—not made of perishable material but hewn stones established and placed by our confession of the Lord Jesus Christ (1 Cor. 3:9-11; 12:18).

But most notably, the Bible describes the Church as a body (1 Cor. 12:12-3; Rom. 12:4-5; Eph. 4:16; Col. 1:18). As you well know, your body is not a loose, disconnected arrangement of parts. You don't leave your arms at work or place your feet into a box for later use. Your body is indivisible and joined together. When your foot is injured, your hands come to the rescue. When your wound is healed, your body rejoices as one. Basically, when you become a Christian, you join the universal Body of Christ. When you become a member of a local church, you apply and walk out that universal union with those Christians who are part of that flock. You show that even though you are an individual under Christ's overall headship, you are also a connected part of the Body of Christ locally. It is in this physical and visual display that believers can unify under the structure, authority, and commitments of Christ and His Word.

Salvation vs. Membership

As stated above, when an individual is saved, he or she becomes a member of the Body of Christ (1 Cor. 12:13). Because they are united to Christ and the other members of the body in this way, they are, therefore, qualified to become a member of a local expression of that universal body.

However, the Scriptures offer a variety of additional,

post-salvation conditions for those establishing and maintaining "membership" or good standing in the local church.

For example, in the New Testament, we see a wide range of roles, responsibilities, moral standards, behavioral expectations, beliefs, processes, and guiding principles to be carried out by those who claim the name of Christ. In fact, those who, after correction, refuse to adhere to these biblical standards are called to be removed from the local church (Matt. 18:15-20; 1 Cor. 5:9-13). Now, removal from the local church is by no means a removal of salvation. That said, it does illustrate the dichotomy of these two realities.

This consistent pattern of local church order and commitment continues throughout the Scriptures and is nurtured and protected by those who the Bible calls elders and deacons (a.k.a. appointed pastors and commissioned servants). Through these two church offices, qualified men shepherd members toward biblical truth, protect members against false doctrine (1 Tim. 3; Titus 1:5-16; Heb. 13:17; 1 Pet. 5:1-4), and serve members according to their needs. Also, the Bible records that elders, in particular, oversee the processes for church discipline, systematic preaching, management of congregational giving, monitoring of relational duties, the maintaining of unity, and more.

Conclusion

Ultimately, this sense of detailed infrastructure affirms God's desire for an orderly and cohesive church (1 Cor.

14:33). I believe it was A.W. Tozer, who pointed out that God's people have always been thoroughly organized. Consider the Israelites and their 613 laws, which brought order to just about everything they did. Consider the placement of Old Testament elders over the people in numerical step (Exod. 18:13-27). Consider the Levitical priesthood by which they facilitated spiritual duties. Consider the Prophets, the Apostles, and even the early church fathers who brought safety to God's people through humble rule and regulation. As nature declares, God is a God of order, and His Church is no different.

Dr. John Muether eloquently reminds us that, "A child without a family is an orphan to be pitied. A man without a country is a refugee to be welcomed. And a Christian without a church is a sheep to be concerned." It has been said, and History confirms it, no new convert to Christianity accepts God's salvation and then wanders around by him or herself, considering if it is wise to assemble with God's Church. The storyline of the Bible and the annals of God's people verify that people repent, get baptized, and make a commitment to the fellowship of a local Christian church (Acts 2:41-47).

So while there is no passage of Scripture that tells Christians, "Thou shalt establish yourself as a local church member," the Bible surely implies and instructs such a commitment. Basically, by entering into faith in Christ, you enter into a covenant with His Church, too. For that reason, we should be willing at some level to publicly state, "I'm a part of this church. While I am here, and until the Lord leads me otherwise, the people at this local church are my people, this man is my pastor, I will do my Christian duties, I will contribute to the financial support of this ministry, and I am willing to be in a reciprocating biblical relationship with those in this flock." For only when every believer is faithful to this kind of commitment to the local church is the universal Church able to live up to her calling as Christ's representative here on earth.

Dale Partridge

President, Relearn.org
October 2019 in Bend, Oregon

Section Two

STATEMENTS

• *Assertio* •

Statements

Statement of Faith

These Statements on Faith, Scripture, The Church, Baptism, and Communion are not originally written content but adapted and/or modernized writings from various historic Christian creeds of the traditional evangelical church.

INTRODUCTION: The Statement of Faith of Relearn. org, is reaffirmed annually by its Board of Directors, theological advisors, faculty, and staff. This statement provides a summary of biblical doctrine that is consistent with historic evangelical Christianity. Additionally, this statement reaffirms many of the doctrinal positions of the common Christian confessions and creeds and identifies our organization not only with the Scriptures but also with the reformers and the evangelical church of our modern era.

Historical creeds affirmed by our ministry include the following: The Apostles' Creed, The Nicene Creed, The 1689 Baptist Confession of Faith, and the Westminster Confession of Faith.

Statement of Faith

WE BELIEVE the Bible is the final standard of faith and practice for the believer in Jesus Christ and for His Church. While recognizing the historical, interpretive and guiding value of creeds and statements of faith made throughout the history of the Church, we affirm the Bible alone as the infallible and final authority in the life of a believer.

WE BELIEVE in the Holy Scriptures as originally given by God, divinely inspired, infallible, entirely trustworthy; and the supreme authority in all matters of faith and conduct; One God, eternally existent in three persons, Father, Son, and Holy Spirit;

WE BELIEVE our Lord Jesus Christ, God manifest in the flesh, His virgin birth, His sinless human life, His divine miracles, His vicarious and atoning death, His bodily resurrection, His ascension, His mediatorial work, and His personal return in power and glory;

WE BELIEVE the Salvation of lost and sinful man through the shed blood of the Lord Jesus Christ by faith apart from works, and regeneration by the Holy Spirit;

WE BELIEVE the Holy Spirit, by Whose indwelling the believer is enabled to live a holy life, to witness and work for the Lord Jesus Christ;

We believe the Unity of the Spirit of all true believers, the Church, the Body of Christ;

We believe the Resurrection of both the saved and the lost; they that are saved unto the resurrection of life, they that are lost unto the resurrection of damnation.

Statements

Statement on Scripture

WE BELIEVE that God has revealed Himself and His truth by both general and special revelation. General revelation displays his existence, power, providence, moral standard, patience, goodness, and glory; special revelation manifests His triune nature and His plan of redemption through Messiah for humanity. This special revelation has been given in various ways, preeminently in the incarnate Word of God, Jesus Christ, and in the inscripturated Word of God, the Bible. We affirm that the sixty-six books of the Bible are the written Word of God given by the Holy Spirit and are the complete and final canonical revelation of God for all time. (Rom. 1:18-2:4; 2:14-16; Ps. 19; Acts 14:15-17; 17:22-31; John 1:1- 18; 1 Thess. 2:13; Heb. 1:1-2; 4:12)

WE BELIEVE these books were written by a process of dual authorship in which the Holy Spirit so moved the human authors that, through their individual personalities and styles, they composed and recorded God's Word which is inerrant. These books, constituting the written Word of God, convey objective truth and are the believer's only infallible rule of faith and practice. (2 Tim. 3:16-17; 2 Pet. 1:19-20; John 10:35; 17:17; 1 Cor. 2:10-13)

WE BELIEVE that, whereas there may be several applications of any given passage of Scripture, there is but one true interpretation. The meaning of Scripture is to be found as one diligently applies the literal grammatical-historical method of interpretation under the enlightenment of the Holy Spirit (John 7:17; 16:12-15; 1 Cor. 2:7-15; 1 John 2:20). It is the responsibility of believers to ascertain carefully the true intent and meaning of Scripture, recognizing that proper application is binding on all generations. Yet the truth of Scripture stands in judgment of men; never do men stand in judgment of it.

Statement on The Church

WE BELIEVE the Church is the people of God, initiated at Pentecost and completed at the return of Christ who is its head. The mission of the Church is to glorify God by worshiping corporately, building itself up as a loving, faithful community by instruction of the Word, observing baptism and communion, embracing the doctrinal mandates of the apostles, communicating the Gospel and making disciples of all peoples. (Matt. 16:18; 28:16-20; Acts 1:4, 5; 11:15; 2:46, 47; 1 Cor. 12:13; Rom. 12:4-21; Eph. 1:22, 23; 2:19-22; 3:4-6; 5:25-27; Col. 1:18; Rev. 5:9)

WE BELIEVE Christians should gather together in local assemblies. They are priests before God and to one another, responsible to serve God and minister to each other. The biblically designated officers serving under Christ and leading the assembly are elders and deacons. Although church and state are distinct institutions, believers are to submit to the government within the limits of God's

Word. (Matt. 18:15-18; 22:15-22; 28:19; Acts 2:41, 42; 6:1-6; 1 Cor. 14:40; Eph. 4:11, 12; 1 Tim. 3:1-13; Tit. 1:5-9; Heb. 10:25; 1 Pet. 2:5-10, 13-17; 5:1-5)

Statement on Baptism and Communion

WE BELIEVE that baptism is an ordinance of the Lord by which those who have repented and come to faith express their union with Christ in His death and resurrection, by being immersed in water in the name of the Father and the Son and the Holy Spirit. It is a sign of belonging to the people of God, and an emblem of burial and cleansing, signifying death to the old life of unbelief, and purification from the pollution of sin. (Matt. 28:16-20; Acts 2:41; 10:47-48; Rom. 6:1-6)

WE BELIEVE that the Lord's Supper is an ordinance of the Lord in which gathered believers eat bread, signifying Christ's body given for His people, and drink the cup of the Lord, signifying the New Covenant in Christ's blood. We do this in remembrance of the Lord, and thus proclaim His death until He comes. This ordinance portrays His death, unites believers in fellowship, and anticipates their participation in the marriage supper of the Lamb. Those who eat and drink in a worthy manner partake of Christ's body and blood, not physically, but spiritually, in that, by faith, they are nourished with the benefits He obtained through His death, and thus grow in grace. (Luke 22:19, 20; 1 Cor. 10:16-18; 11:23-29)

Statements

Statement on Salvation

WE BELIEVE that salvation is wholly of God by grace on the basis of the redemption of Jesus Christ, the merit of His shed blood, and not on the basis of human merit or works (John 1:12; Eph. 1:7; 2:8-10; 1 Pet. 1:18-19).

WE BELIEVE that regeneration is a supernatural work of the Holy Spirit by which the divine nature and divine life are given (John 3:3-7; Tit. 3:5). It is instantaneous and is accomplished solely by the power of the Holy Spirit through the instrumentality of the Word of God (John 5:24) when the repentant sinner, as enabled by the Holy Spirit, responds in faith to the divine provision of salvation. Genuine regeneration is manifested by fruits worthy of repentance as demonstrated in righteous attitudes and conduct. Good works are the proper evidence and fruit of regeneration (1 Cor. 6:19-20; Eph. 2:10), and will be experienced to the extent that the believer submits to the control of the Holy Spirit in his or her life through faithful obedience to the Word of God (Ephesians 5:17-21; Phil. 2:12b; Col. 3:16; 2 Pet. 1:4-10). This obedience causes the believer to be increasingly conformed to the image of our Lord Jesus Christ (2 Cor. 3:18). Such a conformity is climaxed in the believer's glorification at Christ's coming (Rom. 8:17; 2 Pet. 1:4; 1 John 3:2-3).

WE BELIEVE that election is the act of God by which, before the foundation of the world, He chose in Christ those whom He graciously regenerates, saves, and sanctifies (Rom. 8:28-30; Eph. 1:4-11; 2 Thess. 2:13; 2 Tim. 2:10; 1 Pet. 1:1-2). We teach that sovereign election does not contradict or negate the responsibility of man to repent and trust Christ as Savior and Lord (Ezek. 18:23, 32; 33:11; John 3:18-19, 36; 5:40; Rom. 9:22-23; 2 Thess. 2:10-12; Rev. 22:17). Nevertheless, since sovereign grace includes the means of receiving the gift of salvation as well as the gift itself, sovereign election will result in what God determines. All whom the Father calls to Himself will come in faith, and all who come in faith the Father will receive (John 6:37-40, 44; Acts 13:48; James 4:8).

WE BELIEVE that the unmerited favor that God grants to totally depraved sinners is not related to any initiative of their own part or to God's anticipation of what they might do by their own will, but is solely of His sovereign grace and mercy (Eph. 1:4-7; Tit. 3:4-7; 1 Pet. 1:2).

WE BELIEVE that election should not be looked upon

as based merely on abstract sovereignty. God is truly sovereign, but He exercises this sovereignty in harmony with His other attributes, especially His omniscience, justice, holiness, wisdom, grace, and love (Rom. 9:11-16). This sovereignty will always exalt the will of God in a manner totally consistent with His character as revealed in the life of our Lord Jesus Christ (Matt. 11:25-28; 2 Tim. 1:9).

WE BELIEVE that justification before God is an act of God (Rom. 8:33) by which He declares righteous those who, through faith in Christ, repent of their sins (Luke 13:3; Acts 2:38; 3:19; 11:18; Rom. 2:4; 2 Cor. 7:10; Isa. 55:6-7) and confess Him as sovereign Lord (Rom. 10:9-10; 1 Cor. 12:3; 2 Cor. 4:5; Phil. 2:11). This righteousness is apart from any virtue or work of man (Rom. 3:20; 4:6) and involves the imputation of our sins to Christ (Col. 2:14; 1 Pet. 2:24) and the imputation of Christ's righteousness to us (1 Cor. 1:30; 2 Cor. 5:21). By this means God is enabled to "be just and the justifier of the one who has faith in Jesus" (Rom. 3:26).

WE BELIEVE that every believer is sanctified (set apart) unto God by justification and is therefore declared to be holy and is therefore identified as a saint. This sanctification is positional and instantaneous and should not be confused with progressive sanctification. This sanctification has to do with the believer's standing, not his present walk or condition (Acts 20:32; 1 Cor. 1:2, 30;

6:11; 2 Thess. 2:13; Heb. 2:11; 3:1; 10:10, 14; 13:12; 1 Pet. 1:2).

WE BELIEVE that there is also, by the work of the Holy Spirit, a progressive sanctification by which the state of the believer is brought closer to the standing the believer positionally enjoys through justification. Through obedience to the Word of God and the empowering of the Holy Spirit, the believer is able to live a life of increasing holiness in conformity to the will of God, becoming more and more like our Lord Jesus Christ (John 17:17, 19; Rom. 6:1-22; 2 Cor. 3:18; 1 Thess. 4:3-4; 5:23).

In this respect, we teach that every saved person is involved in a daily conflict—the new creation in Christ doing battle against the flesh—but adequate provision is made for victory through the power of the indwelling Holy Spirit. The struggle nevertheless stays with the believer all through this earthly life and is never completely ended. All claims to the eradication of sin in this life are unscriptural. Eradication of sin is not possible, but the Holy Spirit does provide for victory over sin (Gal. 5:16-25; Eph. 4:22-24; Phil. 3:12; Col. 3:9-10; 1 Pet. 1:14-16; 1 John 3:5-9).

WE BELIEVE that all the redeemed, once saved, are kept by God's power and are thus secure in Christ forever (John 5:24; 6:37-40; 10:27-30; Rom. 5:9-10; 8:1, 31-39; 1 Cor. 1:4-8; Eph. 4:30; Heb. 7:25; 13:5; 1 Pet. 1:5; Jude 24).

WE BELIEVE that it is the privilege of believers to rejoice

in the assurance of their salvation through the testimony of God's Word, which, however, clearly forbids the use of Christian liberty as an occasion for sinful living and carnality (Rom. 6:15-22; 13:13-14; Gal. 5:13, 25-26; Tit. 2:11-14).

WE BELIEVE that separation from sin is clearly called for throughout the Old and New Testaments, and that the Scriptures clearly indicate that in the last days apostasy and worldliness shall increase (2 Cor. 6:14-7:1; 2 Tim. 3:1-5).

WE BELIEVE that, out of deep gratitude for the undeserved grace of God granted to us, and because our glorious God is so worthy of our total consecration, all the saved should live in such a manner as to demonstrate our adoring love to God and so as not to bring reproach upon our Lord and Savior. We also believe that separation from all religious apostasy and worldly and sinful practices is commanded of us by God (Rom. 12:1-2, 1 Cor. 5:9-13; 2 Cor. 6:14-7:1; 1 John 2:15-17; 2 John 9-11).

WE BELIEVE that believers should be separated unto our Lord Jesus Christ (2 Thess. 1:11-12; Heb. 12:1-2) and affirm that the Christian life is a life of obedient righteousness that reflects the teaching of the Beatitudes (Matt. 5:2-12) and a continual pursuit of holiness (Rom. 12:1-2; 2 Cor. 7:1; Heb. 12:14; Tit. 2:11-14; 1 John 3:1-10).[1]

Section Three

DOCTRINES

• *Dogma* •

Introduction

Church Doctrines

*"Till I come, give attention to reading, to
exhortation, to doctrine."*

1ST TIMOTHY 4:13

Church doctrines are simply the central themes of God's revelation for church practice found in Scripture. This is no exhaustive list. However, we believe these ten articles summarize our interpretation and convictions regarding the local church.

While the talk of doctrine can seem intimidating and intellectual, these beliefs are not without purpose. Together, these doctrines create a spiritual destination—a church culture that's built upon the Word of God.

In developing this collection of dogma, our objective was to establish an ecclesiology that can be adopted and endorsed by all evangelical house churches in all locations. We believe the Bible's call for local church practice is universal; therefore, it cannot be inhibited by any other factors which can differ from culture to culture.

While we believe in the freedom to add extra-curricular, biblically-aligned practices (youth programs, membership classes, worship bands, etc.) to the local church expression, we do not believe these personalized demonstrations can be considered doctrinal or required. In fact, in some cases, they have proven harmful. We believe the Bible's prescription for local church practice must be transnational and cross-cultural. It must be possible in a persecuted country as well as a supportive one. It must be possible in the poorest of nations as well as the highest peaks of society. Like the Gospel, any version of church assembly that is not usable and accessible by all, cannot be purely biblical. That is to say, any version that requires a building or congregational affluence or salaried staff or religious freedom or higher education or civil peace is imposing extra-biblical preferences onto the biblical design for local Christian assembly.

Below, you will find the Relearn.org doctrines for the local church. We believe they are each wholly supported by Scripture and, together, form a fruitful and holy gathering of believers who glorify God in their local community.

Church Doctrines

Articles

Article 01. Church

We believe there is one holy Church of Jesus Christ seen in two distinct forms—local and universal (Rom 12:5; 1 Cor. 12:20; 1 Tim. 3:15). The first includes professing believers in Jesus Christ, who assemble in a biblically-ordered congregation at a particular location on a regular basis. The second includes all professing believers in Jesus Christ (past, present, and future) living across the globe.

We believe in the autonomy of the local church, free from any external authority or control, with the right of self-government and freedom from the interference of any hierarchy of individuals or organizations (Tit. 1:5). We teach that it is scriptural for true churches to cooperate with each other for the presentation and propagation of the faith. Each local church, however, through its elders and their interpretation and application of Scripture, should be the sole judge of the measure and method of its cooperation. The elders should determine all other matters of membership, policy, discipline, benevolence, and government as well (Acts 15:19–31; 20:28; 1 Cor. 5:4–7, 13; 1 Pet. 5:1–4).[2]

Article 02. Mission

We believe the mission of the Church is threefold: First, it is to edify and nourish its members through biblical doctrine, spiritual gifts, and relational duties of love (Eph. 4:11-16; Romans 12:3-21; 1 Cor. 12). Second, it is to go into the world and proclaim the Gospel and make disciples of Jesus Christ through the power of the Spirit (Matt. 28:16-20). Third, it is to be the demonstration of the Gospel—it's power, fruitfulness, and hope to an onlooking world (Matt. 5:13-16; 1 Peter 3:15). Through edification, proclamation, and demonstration, the Lord will build His Church (Matt. 16:18) and gather these disciples into local communities (1 Cor. 12:18) where they can worship, obey, and grow in Jesus Christ until the Day of His return. This threefold mission of the Church is to be distinct from the purpose of the Church, which is to glorify God (Eph. 3:21).

Article 03. People

We believe the Church of Jesus Christ is not a place but a people—the Body of Christ, of which He is the head (Eph. 1:22–23) and Chief Shepherd (1 Pet. 5:4). Furthermore, we believe the local church is the assembly of God's redeemed and baptized people for the *central* purpose of edification and worship and not for the purpose of evangelism and outreach to unbelievers (2 Cor. 6:14; Eph 4:11-12). That said, we do not believe in forbidding unbelievers from attending a local assembly as the Lord may direct an individual for the purpose of hearing the Gospel through the preaching of the Word of God. (1 Cor. 14:24-25; Rom. 10:17).

Article 04. Evangelism

We believe evangelism is the central *outward* ministry of the local church and its members. It is the walking out of the Great Commission by proclamation of the Gospel of Jesus Christ that leads unto salvation. It is an outreach ministry with the aim and hope to persuade, convince, convert, and disciple. We believe this ministry is the responsibility of every Christian and is not to be neglected or outsourced to the leaders of the local church.

Article 05. Unity

We believe Jesus Christ calls His Church to extravagant unity (John 17:20-23). In speaking to the local church, we believe unity is brought forth by a sharing of our common faith in Jesus Christ through the lens of Scripture (1 Cor. 1:10). We believe this spiritual unity is achieved not through human endeavoring but only by the work of the Holy Spirit in the life of individual believers (Eph. 4:3-6; 1 Cor. 12:13). Moreover, we believe the substance of local church unity is generated primarily by the alignment of our theological beliefs, our mutually edifying spiritual gifts, and the fulfillment of the "one-another's" seen in Scripture (1 Cor. 12; Rom.12:15; Phil. 2:2; Rom. 15:1-5).

It is worth mentioning, while unity in the matters of scriptural authority, Christology, and the Gospel is imperative, we do not believe that local church unity requires complete theological uniformity. We believe the local church must provide latitude in non-essential doctrines, worship style, and personal spiritual demonstration as long as they do not violate the Holy Scriptures. We believe through this freedom of spiritual expression, a diverse assembly of believers can remain supernaturally united under the headship of Christ (1 Cor 12:12).

Article 06. Meeting

We believe a church meeting is a formally declared assembly of local church members for the purpose of worship (e.g., the Sunday gathering). We believe the meeting is to be conducted under the doctrines of orderly worship found in 1 Corinthians 11:17-34; 12; 14:26-40, 1 Timothy 2:1-15; 3-4, and Titus 1-3. While there are additional passages that speak to the local church, we believe these central ecclesiastical passages form up a majority of the doctrine regarding local assembly. That is, they beckon for a contributor-centric, Holy Spirit-led, gender role-invoked, elder-governed, edification-focused, and orderly Christian assembly.

In the matter of preaching (*further discussed in Convictions 02-03*), we align with the 1689 *Baptist Confession of Faith* which states, "Although it be incumbent on the bishops or pastors of the churches to be instant in preaching the word, by way of office, yet the work of preaching the word is not so peculiarly confined to them but that others also gifted and fitted by the Holy Spirit for it, and approved and called by the church, may and ought to perform it."[3] (1 Pet. 4:10-11; 1 Cor. 14:26-33). Additionally, we view the historical, four-part pattern (teaching doctrine, fellowship, breaking bread, and prayer) of the early church assembly seen in Acts 2:42 as a broad, yet instructive example for the structure of a local church assembly.

In accordance with Scripture, while all are to come to the church gathering spiritually postured, we believe men are to come spiritually prepared. That is, men are encouraged to be in both prayer and study prior to the assembled meeting with the expectation that the Holy Spirit may lead them to share an edifying truth, prayer, teaching, song of praise, or revelation during the assembly. Moreover, we believe the Apostle Paul voiced his preference concerning prayer in the local church and that it is to be carried out by the men, "I desire therefore that the men pray everywhere, lifting up holy hands, without wrath and doubting…" (1 Tim. 2:8). In summation, we believe the weekly church meeting is the venue God has chosen for men to display His spiritual authority structure (Eph. 5:22-33; 1 Cor. 11:3; 1 Tim. 2:12-14; Gen. 3:16) and exercise their spiritual gifts under the oversight of qualified elders for the building up of the church (Rom. 12:6-8; 1 Pet. 4:10-11; 1 Cor. 12; Eph. 4:11-16).

With regard to a woman's role during church meetings, we adhere to the doctrines seen in 1 Corinthians 14:34-

35 and 1 Timothy 2:8-12. While we do not believe the text is commanding a complete prohibition of women participating in the church meeting, we do believe the text prohibits women from teaching, preaching, exhorting, prophesying, contending over doctrine, and assuming spiritual authority during this specific period of time. We do believe, however, the Scriptures permit women (during the church gathering) to sing, share personal testimonies, voice prayer requests, and make church-related announcements. We believe these gender role doctrines are not for the purpose of female oppression but rather God's means to protect the church from false doctrine (1 Tim. 2:12-14), display creation order (1 Cor. 11:8-10), preserve the authority structure for the family (Eph. 5:22-33), and protect against male spiritual passivity (Gen. 3:6-13.). Having said that, it's important to affirm that we believe women are equally valuable before God but different in role in the local church assembly. Likewise, we do not believe women are bound to these ecclesiastical doctrines outside of the local church meeting. In fact, we believe God gifts and equips women for a variety of ministries from gospel preaching (Mark 6:9-10; Matt. 28:16-20) and spontaneous prophesying (1 Cor 11:15; Acts 21:7-9) to female discipleship (Tit. 2:3-5), music, and church hospitality (Col. 4:15).

In relation to children in the church meeting, we believe Scripture instructs families to worship together. Otherwise stated, we do not believe the Bible encourages children's church or Sunday School. We believe the responsibility of child discipleship is to be strictly carried out by parents (Deut. 6:6-7; Eph. 6:4; Prov. 22:6; Col 3:20-21). That said, children (excluding babies) are expected to be taught and trained to sit quietly and observe others and their parents during the church assembly.

For a more practical and functional view of this doctrine, see section five on "Free-Worship Liturgy."

Article 07. Worship

What the modern church has identified as worship, the Bible has identified as *songs of praise* (Ps. 68:4; Ps. 69:30; Ps 95:1-11; Ps. 147:1;). In that regard, corporate, musical praise is a form of worship, and for that reason, should conform to the biblical instruction for such activity. In John 4:24-25 it states, "But the hour is coming, and now is, when the true worshipers will worship the Father in *spirit and truth*; for the Father is seeking such to worship Him. God is Spirit, and those who worship Him must worship in spirit and truth" (italics added for emphasis). This principle of compounding heart-centered worship with biblical-centered truth speaks thunderously that the worship of God, whether by prayer or by preaching or by singing, must be done properly and in alignment with the Word of God.

In the early happenings of the reformation, Martin Luther established what's now called the *normative principle of worship*. In short, this means that a congregation will not do anything forbidden by Scripture. That said, this perspective offers an open door to a wide variety of church and worship expressions that, throughout church history, has proven unfruitful and even dangerous. We believe it is not enough to simply *not do* what is forbidden by Scripture; we believe we *must do* what is commanded in Scripture and nothing more. For that reason, we adopt what the church has called the *regulative principle of worship*. That is, we believe a congregation may only do that which is commanded in Scripture. It is from this place that we worship God as He commanded not as we desire (Gen. 4:3–8; Exod. 25:40; Deut. 12:4; 1 Sam. 15:22; Matt. 15:1–14; Col. 2:18;).

This holy and obedient expectation is a sister to Jesus's three-part command, "Love the Lord your God with all your heart, with all your soul, and with all your mind." (Matt. 22:37). Ultimately, we believe a congregation learns their theology not only by the preaching they hear but by the prayers they pray and by the songs they sing. The Apostle Paul furthers this idea of truth-bound praise and worship in 1 Corinthians 14:15 where he states, "I will pray with the spirit, and I will also pray with the understanding. I will sing with the spirit, and I will also sing with the understanding." In short, we do not believe in accommodating worship music that takes such creative license that it causes theological confusion and misunderstanding. That is, we believe the same doctrinal accuracy that is expected of a preacher's sermon is to be applied to a worship musician's song lyrics (Jam. 3:1; 1 Pet. 4:11).

Lastly, we believe a congregation's behavior during worship is to be orderly and exhibiting the fruits of the Spirit, including self-control (1 Cor. 14:33; Gal. 5:22-23; 2 Tim. 1:7). Now, that does not mean that members cannot express their devotion to God through passionate praise or the raising of hands and voices, but it does mean that we do so in a way that maintains harmony with the congregation and reverence before God.

Article 08. Governance

We believe there are only two offices that constitute biblical church government: Elders and Deacons. These are two separate offices with separate responsibilities. To put it briefly, elders fulfill the spiritual shepherding duties while deacons attend to the physical needs of the flock. Below is a brief overview of both offices and how they relate to the congregation.

Elder: In the New Testament, we see a variety of words used to describe this office—"elder" (*presbuteros*), "overseer" (*episkopos*), and "pastor" (*poim̄en*). While the modern church most commonly uses the latter term (pastor) to identify this position, we will learn that Scripture uses all three of these terms to describe this one office. To support this doctrinal perspective, 1 Timothy 3:1-7 presents the qualifications for an overseer (*episkopos*) which are nearly identical to the qualifications for an elder (*presbuteros*) in Titus 1:6-9. In fact, in the passage seen in Titus 1, Paul uses both of these terms in reference to the same office (*presbuteros* in v. 5 and *episkopos* in v. 7). Additionally, in both Acts 20 and 1 Peter 5:1-2, we see all three of these words used interchangeably throughout the text. In short, these three words used in Scripture are not to identify three different offices but to showcase the variety of ministerial duties involved within the singular office of Elder.[4]

Qualifications and Responsibilities: To preface, Jesus Christ is the ultimate Shepherd of His Church. However, in Scripture, He has commissioned and appointed under-shepherds (elders) to guide, feed, and protect His local flocks (Acts 20:28). For this reason, 1 Timothy 3:2-7 and Titus 1:6-8 demand the highest requirements of character for the men who fulfill this spiritual office. As a central qualification, elders are to be married men with children whom are old enough to display their submission and obedience to their father. As 1 Timothy 3:5 clearly states, "For if a man does not know how to rule his own house, how will he take care of the church of God?"

In terms of spiritual responsibilities, their chief duties are to both preach sound doctrine and protect against false doctrine. As a result, the office of Elder is the highest level of local church leadership and carries the greatest amount of spiritual responsibility (Heb. 13:17).

As a caretaker of the local church, these overseers of the flock are to determine church policy (Acts 15:22); oversee the church (Acts 20:28); appoint others for church government (Titus 1:5); rule, teach, and preach (1 Tim. 5:17; cf. 1 Thess. 5:12; 1 Tim. 3:2). They are to exhort and refute (Titus 1:9). But at the heart, they are to act as shepherds, directing, and setting an example for all (1 Pet. 5:1-3).[5]

In relation to the congregation, Scripture calls for the members of a local church to recognize and esteem (1 Thess. 5:12-13), spiritually submit and emulate (Heb. 13:7; Heb. 13:17; 1 Pet. 5:5-6), grant honor and financially support (1 Tim. 5:17-18), and to not receive an accusation against them without the presence of two or three witnesses (1 Tim. 5:19-20). Furthermore, the congregation is to hold these individuals to the strict standards of Scripture while also extending grace and understanding in times of repentant error. While these men serve a vital role in the local church, it is important to state that their authority is spiritual and not physical. These men are to be revered and respected, but they are not to be viewed as possessing control of any particular church member's personal decisions, family, or resources.

Deacon: The Greek word *diakonos* is translated to "deacon" in the English language and means "servant" or "minister" (Rom. 15:8; 1 Cor. 3:5; Cor. 3:6; Col 1:23). This word is used in a variety of passages in Scripture to reference servanthood or acts of church service (Matt. 20:26; Acts 11:29; 12:25; 19:22; Rom. 15:31; 2 Cor. 8:4; 9:1, 12, 13). Having said that, this is not an examination of its verb presentation but its noun format (1 Tim. 8-13; Eph. 6:21; 1 Thess. 3:2;). That is, there is a Christian duty of service and then there is the office of formalized Church Servant.

Deacons do not replace the scriptural requirement of church members to serve one another. However, they are a great additional benefit to a local church and should be honored and respected for their humble service.

Qualifications and Responsibilities: The qualifications for these commissioned servants can be found in 1 Timothy 3:8-13. Unlike the office of elder, the deacon's responsibilities are limited to local church servanthood and not to interfere with congregational shepherding. In essence, the deacons are authorized individuals utilized by the elder(s) to accommodate and organize meeting the physical needs of the local congregation. This may include spiritual encouragement, informational meetings, hospitality, baptism, the facilitation of the Lord's Supper, financial burdens, lodging, personal sustenance, health requirements, and emergencies. Biblically speaking, it is the deacons who help diversify the physical demands of the flock from the elder(s) to ensure their efforts of spiritual leadership, study, and preaching can remain uninterrupted (Acts 6:1-4).

We believe, according to Scripture, that formalized and appointed deacons are to be married men with children. 1 Timothy 3:11-12 states, "Likewise, their wives must be reverent, not slanderers, temperate, faithful in all things. Let deacons be the husbands of one wife, ruling their children and their own houses well." As previously stated, we believe all Christians are called to serve the church; however, the Scriptures make an indicated difference between a Christian's common service and the office of Deacon. In 1 Timothy 3:10 the text states, "But let these also first be tested; then let them serve as deacons, being found blameless." This testing and examination prior to service imply a clear distinction between the universal service all Christians are called to perform and the special service to be carried out by proven and appointed Deacons. While some have used the argument of Phoebe in Romans 16:1 who is referenced as a deacon in the local church to justify female Deacons, we believe, since the word *diakonos* (which is used 29 times in the New Testament) simply means *servant*, Paul used this term as a description of her fervent Christian service to the local church and not as an identifying term of her formalized church office.

Article 09. Discipline

We believe church discipline is God's mode of purification for His church and His method for the protection of His reputation in the world. In fact, history confirms, discipline must be exercised in the Church, for, without it, it would soon look like the culture. We believe any person who identifies themselves as a Christian is to be held to the spiritual and moral standards of that public profession set forth in the Scriptures (Rom. 16:17-18; 2 Thess. 3:13-15; 2 John 1:9-10). The letter of 1 Corinthians clearly supports this belief when it states, "But now I have written to you not to keep company with anyone named a brother [or sister], who is sexually immoral, or covetous, or an idolater, or a reviler, or a drunkard, or an extortioner—

not even to eat with such a person" (5:11). This passage goes on to say, "Is it not those inside the church whom you are to judge? God judges those outside. 'Purge the evil person from among you'" (5:12-13). In short, Christians are not to tolerate brothers and sisters walking in known, unrepentant sin. As a matter of fact, we are not even to associate with these individuals unless it is for the explicit purpose of exhortation (Gal. 6:1; 2 Thess. 3:13-15). In the Gospels, The Lord Himself furthers the demand for church discipline by giving us a very specific process for dealing with those in the local church who are caught in personal or public sin.

In Matthew 18:15-17, He says, "Moreover if your brother sins against you, go and tell him his fault between you and him alone. If he hears you, you have gained your brother. But if he will not hear, take with you one or two more, that 'by the mouth of two or three witnesses every word may be established.' And if he refuses to hear them, tell it to the church. But if he refuses even to hear the church, let him be to you like a heathen and a tax collector."

The Lord's grace continues to shine forth as we see His model uphold an obvious progression from gentle private correction to harsh public ex-communication. Regardless of the stage of discipline and correction, our deepest hope, as Christians, should always be for full restoration (2 Cor. 2:5-11; Jam. 5:19-20). Additionally, it is never to be a joy to inflict correction or church discipline but a duty as a brother or sister in Christ (1 Cor. 5:2). Nonetheless, it is worth stating that in the case of a personal offense, the Scriptures do teach that it is both to our glory to overlook a personal transgression (Prov. 19:11) and to our dignity to allow our love for another Christian to cover a multitude of sins (1 Pet. 4:8). That being said, we believe it is not loving to overlook a pattern of sin or dangerous moral failure that is damaging to them, others, or to the reputation of Christ and His Church.

We believe correction in connection to personal offense is a shared duty of all church members. However, we believe more advanced or serious cases of church discipline fall upon the shoulders of the elders of the church as they are called, by Scripture, to give an account of the spiritual status of the flock to Christ (Heb. 13:17).

Lastly, we believe correction and church discipline are vital parts of a biblical house church, and every church member should expect to experience a moment of correction as long as they are in scripturally-guided community with other believers. According to Scripture, this experience of correction should produce humility, repentance, restoration, and gratitude (Prov. 9:8; Prov. 11:2; Prov. 12:15; Luke 17:3-4; Heb. 12:11; Jam. 4:6). In fact, the Bible tells us that only a fool despises correction (Prov. 1:7; Prov. 27:5-6). In closing, church discipline is to be viewed as a blessing. To have a community of people acting as guard rails and protecting one's spiritual health, the state of their family, and their status within the church is a tremendous benefit to the Christian life.

Article 10. Giving

We believe church members are strongly encouraged by Scripture to financially participate in three forms of giving. (1) Giving to the poor (Prov. 19:17; Prov. 22:9; Matt. 5:42; Luke 12:33; Matt. 25:35-45; Matt. 19:21; Mark 12:41-44;). (2) Giving to the local and global needs of the saints (1 John 3:17; Heb. 13:16; Rom. 12:13; Jam. 2:15-16; Gal. 6:2; 1 Cor. 16:1-4). (3) Giving to the elders who fulfill spiritual labors for the benefit of the local congregation (1 Cor. 9:5-12; Luke 10:7; 1 Tim. 5:18; Gal. 6:6, Jam. 5:4-5). Additionally, we believe the New Testament's call for generosity has superseded the Old Testament's call for tithing. We, as New Covenant Christians, are not under the jurisdiction of the Old Covenant (Eph. 2:15; Gal. 2:19) and, as a result, are relieved from the command of tithing to the Levite priesthood and to the ministerial needs of the temple. Instead, we are commanded to be generous with one another under the law of love (2 Corinthians 9:6-8). We do believe giving, in any format, is a private matter only to be known by those who give and receive and by the Lord (Matt. 6:3-4). While we do not believe an unwillingness to give is grounds for church discipline, we do believe Christians who refuse to contribute to the ministry and shepherds in which they directly benefit is an incorrect and immature spiritual posture that should be brought before the Lord in prayer.

In the format of a local church that meets in a home, giving to the ministry and shepherds can vary. Additionally, one should not expect a tax benefit for their gift as most home gatherings are not formalized tax-exempt organizations. That said, some countries like the United States allow for tax-deductible gifts up to $15,000.00 per year per recipient.[6] Please look to your federal laws for instruction in this matter.

In general, church shepherds should make it clear to the church members regarding a preferred process of giving. For some churches, it might be an offering box in the home; for others, it may be accomplished electronically or by check or cash in person. Regardless of the elected financial vehicle, giving should be made clear by the shepherd but pursued by the individual church member.

As for giving to others in the local church, it is the responsibility of the members to present their needs publicly or privately so they may be met.

For more information to support this theological perspective on giving, consider reading "Why Tithing is Biblical but it's Not Christian" which can be read at Relearn.org

Section Four

CONVICTIONS

• *Coargutio* •

Introduction

Church Convictions

*"The faith which you have, have as your own
conviction before God. Happy is he who does not
condemn himself in what he approves."*

Romans 14:22

It was Martin Luther who said to violate one's conscience
is neither right or safe. Different from the previous
section's doctrines, these church convictions are matters
of conscience and scriptural interpretations. While many,
if not most historic Christian churches would align with
this perspective, these are peripheral preferences based on
biblical principles, not specific commands of Scripture.

However, these convictions have not simply been
helpful to our small network of churches; they have
also been fruitful. Within these convictions, are much
of the makings of the rich biblical culture our ministry
champions. Additionally, we, as a network of church
planters, elders, and theologians, have bore witness of the
positive evidence that has resulted from their application
in the local house church setting.

Church Convictions

Articles

Article 01. Appointment

While an exact process is not presented in Scripture, we believe the New Testament displays a clear set of five chronological events for the appointment of elders and deacons in the local church.

1. Gifting: A man has an evident spiritual gift for teaching, pastoral care, and serving (1 Cor. 12:7-11; 1 Tim 3:1; Eph. 4:11).

2. Qualifying: A man meets the biblical qualifications for the office (1 Tim. 3:1-13; Tit. 1:5-9).

3. Anointing: A man, through personal conviction and demonstration of that conviction within the congregation is called by God to the office (Acts 20:28; Eph. 4:11-12).

4. Recognizing: A man, through congregational recognition and validation, is selected to fill the office (Acts 6:3).

5. Appointing: A man, by the power of the congregation through the laying on of hands by the men of the church, is appointed to the office (Acts 14:23; Tit. 1:5).

In an effort to maintain ecclesiological purity and unity, elders and deacons of local assemblies who desire to be formally included in our community of Relearn.org churches are required to accept the teachings found within this Relearn.org Doctrines and Convictions document.

Article 02. Expository Teaching

We believe it should be the aim of those shepherding or teaching in the local church to centralize and prioritize expository teaching over topical teaching. That is, any sermon or teaching should find its sole source of the content in Scripture, and the substance of the teaching should be retrieved through careful exegesis and proper hermeneutics. Furthermore, expositors seek to align the interpretation of the biblical text within the larger doctrinal truths seen throughout Scripture. Moreover, teachers will always connect their sermon to the Bible's greater narrative and present how Christ, the final fulfillment of the text, is the central focus of all Scripture.

We also believe that a church who is convicted to proclaim all of Scripture will never allow any significant portion of the Bible to be ignored. In Acts 20:27, Paul declares, "for I did not shrink from declaring to you the whole counsel of God." For this reason, we believe it is right for shepherds and teachers to direct their preaching efforts in a systematic, verse-by-verse format that does not avoid certain passages of Scripture due to unpopularity, lack of cultural comfort, or complexity.

Because God's Word is what converts, convicts, edifies, corrects, and sanctifies those in the Church (Heb. 4:12; Rom. 10:17; 1 Pet. 1:23; 1 Thess. 2:13; John. 17:17), elders, preachers, and teachers must make Scripture the center of the sermon. In short, the goal of the expository preacher is not to hear, "What a great sermon" or "What an uplifting message" but to hear from their church members, "Thank you, I now understand what that biblical passage means and how it applies to my life."

Article 03. Biblical Theology

We believe both elders and church members should have a firm understanding of biblical theology. That is, we believe the strength and health of a local church is dependent upon its individual members comprehending the arrangement and agreement of the Scriptures as one unified story (1 Tim. 1:5, 2 John 1-6, and Titus 2:1-10). When a church establishes a doctrinal culture of biblical theology, members will prevent any individual portions of Scripture from being extracted and interpreted from the whole. Instead, both preachers and members will recognize that all Scripture, while organized in covenants and books and chapters, is one consistent and historically revealed plan of redemption culminating in the birth, ministry, death, resurrection, and ascension of Jesus Christ.

Article 04. Houses

While a biblical church meeting can theoretically take place anywhere (a garage, under a tree, in a building, etc.), we are convicted that the house offers the most effective setting to generate the intimacy, closeness, and security required to walk out the level of love seen between church members in the New Testament. Some argue that the New Testament Christians only met in homes because they could not gather elsewhere. While this is partially true in a pragmatic sense, we do not believe that having access to public buildings today should decrease the biblical example and benefits of house gatherings found in the Scriptures (Acts 2:46; Acts 5:42; 20:20 ; 1 Cor. 16:19; Rom. 16:5; Col. 4:15; Phil. 1:2).

Furthermore, and most beneficially, meeting in homes forces groups to be small and deeply connected while also encouraging the sense of family that seems to be missing between most Christians today. Lastly, and more practically speaking, house gatherings alleviate the legalities of incorporation, reduce the risk of persecution (for those living in hostile areas), and eliminate the massive financial weight of a church building and operations. In short, because church members already have homes available to them, the money allocated for a traditional church venue can be reinvested into other spiritual needs.

We believe it is beneficial but not mandatory for house churches to rotate homes at some predetermined frequency (e.g., every eight weeks). Ideally, the act of hosting and serving the local church should be a shared activity not to be absorbed strictly by the elders or by one or two families. However, because hosting is an indirect form of church influence, we believe it should not be carried out by those young in their faith or new to a particular assembly. Additionally, each local church will be limited to the geography, parking, liabilities, and square footage of the homes within its gathering.

> **Suggestion:** In connection to homes, we have found it beneficial but not necessary for churches to create a church-hosting kit complete with folding chairs, pulpit, songbooks, and dishware. Some gatherings have even included a guitar, communion set, and extra Bibles.

Article 05. Fellowship

The word *fellowship* is a term that has been vandalized by the Western Church. In other words, we have distorted it into an expression that has lost much of its original meaning. The Greek word for fellowship is *koinonia [koi·no·nia]*, and it does not merely signify Christian friendship or even Christian gathering. Biblically speaking, *koinonia* is displayed as an interactive, reciprocating, and participating relationship with both God and believers who share in their mutual new-life through Christ (Acts 2:42; 1 John 1:3, 6–7; 2 Cor. 9:13; Phil. 3:10).

That is to say, to experience biblical fellowship is to engage in the sharing of both spiritual giving and spiritual receiving. It is the spiritual ethic that while we may have no secular attributes in common (where we live, what we enjoy, our ethnicity, our age, etc.), we can still find and experience rich exchanging of fellowship through our joint faith in Jesus Christ.

Furthermore, we believe true fellowship is anchored in intentional relationship. Namely, biblical fellowship cannot take root in a local church that nurtures "audience Christianity" or "spectator Christianity." The Bible is clear that church members are to purpose themselves to contribute and reciprocate with one another in love. It is through this self-denying, one-anothering, servanthood-centered culture that we can eradicate the all-too-common spirit of independence that plagues many of today's churches. For this reason, we believe local churches should strive to cultivate fellowship by allowing for time not only during the Sunday assembly but also throughout the week. We believe that genuine fellowship must integrate daily by weaving itself into a rich communal culture on mission for the Gospel.

Suggestion: We have found it fruitful but not mandatory for local churches to host mid-week, mission-focused men's gatherings, and women's gatherings. This layer of intentional fellowship time greatly strengthens the bond between believers and allows for a more united meeting on Sunday.

Article 06. Discipleship

As part of the Great Commission (Matt. 28:18-20), Christians are to make disciples. This does not mean we are called to produce disciples in our way of Christianity. Rather, we are commanded to create and strengthen disciples of Christ. We believe, however, the work of discipleship is first accomplished through the preaching and hearing of God's Word (Rom. 10:17) and secondly through Christian fellowship, encouragement, accountability, and intercessory prayer (Hebrews 10:24-25).

In the local church setting, while we believe the elders are primarily responsible for church-wide discipleship through preaching, we also believe one-on-one discipleship in its many forms (evangelism, teaching, guiding, praying, correcting, exhorting, and encouraging) is the duty of every Christian. That said, while the Scriptures call men to lead the church as a whole, we, by a complementarian conviction and alignment with the *Danvers Statement of Biblical Manhood and Womanhood*, maintain that women are called to lead the women and men are called to lead men in their interpersonal relationships.[7]

Furthermore, we believe this one-on-one discipleship is to be ordered according to spiritual maturity, age, and biblical role. For example, Titus 2:1-10 commands proper examples of older men to be displayed for the younger men and for older women to teach younger women how to love their husbands and their children.

Lastly, we believe parents are to be the leading source

of discipleship for their children, but they are not to be the only source. In our judgment, the warning of Matthew 18:6 is to be seriously considered in any discipleship activity but especially in the discipleship of a young believer, "But whoever causes one of these little ones who believe in Me to sin, it would be better for him if a millstone were hung around his neck, and he were drowned in the depth of the sea." Discipleship in the local church is a weighty and consequential assignment in which all Christians are to engage with a pure heart and a yielded spirit to God's Word.

Article 07. Outreach

God, through the Great Commission (Matt. 28:18-20), has called the members of His Church to the work of evangelism and outreach. However, we believe the term "outreach" more accurately describes the pragmatic nature of this crucial ministry—which is outward. That is, we believe evangelism is an external ministry of the local church and not internal. We, as members of a local church, are called to share the verbal Gospel (Rom. 10:17; Matt. 28:18-20) through all means available to us as an assembly of God's people.

Nevertheless, we do not believe Christians should invite their unsaved friends to the local church meeting as a way to offload their spiritual responsibility of Gospel sharing to their pastor or others within their church community. According to Scripture, evangelism is the work of every Christian (2 Cor. 5:18-20; Matt. 5:14-16; 1 Pet. 3:15; Phil.

2:14-16; Col. 4:5-6; 1 Pet. 2:9). We, as individual believers, are to pray the Lord grants us each opportunities both publicly and in our private relationships to share His Gospel faithfully. In the event we experience a person who displays the genuine fruits of conversion, we believe, we are to follow the biblical example of promptly baptizing that individual, discipling that individual through the teaching of God's Word, and inviting that individual to gather with the people of God in the local church (Matt. 28:18-20).

Having said that, we do not believe in human-led Gospel promotion. Throughout the Scriptures, those who preached publicly were led by the Spirit and those who preached privately were led by the Spirit (1 Thess. 1:5; 1 Pet. 1:12; Acts 4:8-12; 6:10 13:4-5; 16:6; 1 Cor. 2:4-5; 2:13; John 14:26). We are not to turn God's mission of evangelism into man's efforts of soul-saving. We believe the Lord calls each of us to be prepared, ready, and willing to share the Good News with others (2 Tim. 4:2, 1 Pet. 3:15; 2 Cor. 5:17-19). With this biblical perspective, we can trust that God's ministry will never compromise His other commands regarding marriage, family, friendships, finances, and church. God, who has perfect will, will remove any obstacles and prepare all paths for His message to be heard.

Article 08. Guests

One might wonder why a process for inviting guests to a church gathering is so important that it demanded an entire article in this document? If you share in this curiosity, it is likely a result of your westernized perspective of the local church. For those planting, leading, and attending underground house churches in persecuted countries, however, invitation, and the process of it, is critical. Church members should know not only the biblical parameters of church invitation but also the scriptural wisdom that can uphold order, physical safety, and the spiritual health for those already in the local flock.

Due to the nature of an every-member-functioning gathering, it's important to recognize that any member is permitted to invite guests and any invited guest is biblically permitted to participate in the meeting in some way. Additionally, these guests will also be brought into the presence of the church's children and the personal home and life of the church member hosting at that particular time. For this reason, we believe it is very important to first determine if visitors are authentic believers and not persecutors, false teachers, or wolves in sheep's clothing.

We will separate our suggested process of invitation into three groups:

Unbelievers: The local church, the Body of Christ, is first and foremost an assembly of believers for the edification of believers. Nonetheless, we are not to prohibit unbelievers from attending the local church meeting (1 Cor. 14:24-25). However, the allowing of unbelievers in the local assembly and a church culture that encourages members to invite unbelievers is very different. As stated in our conviction regarding outreach, evangelism, such as Gospel preaching and baptizing, is presented scripturally as an outward ministry of the individual Christian and not an inward ministry of the local church in its corporate expression. That is to say, we believe inviting unbelievers to the local church meeting is to put things in the wrong order. Scripture declares that the common process of conversion and baptism precedes the attachment and membership in the local church. Now, if an unbeliever is led by the Holy Spirit to show up to a local church meeting, we are to embrace this person and allow them to see the power of God in the presence of His people (1 Cor. 14:24-25).

As it pertains to the invitation of confessed and baptized Christians, we believe it's useful to break these guests into two groups: Non-Local Visitors and Local Potential Members.

Non-Local Visitors: All church members at some point will be presented with Christian friends or family who has found themselves in town during your Sunday home gathering. If these friends have an interest in attending your house church, bring them. However, our experience has taught us that many Christians have never experienced a biblical house church assembly and may be uncomfortable with church doctrine regarding gender roles or children being present or even certain sermon content. For that reason, we suggest setting theological and structural expectations with your guests prior to the church meeting. We also recommend notifying the members of your church as a courtesy as it does change the intimacy of the meeting.

Local Potential Members: 1 Corinthians 12:18 boldly states, "But now God has set the members, each one of them, in the body just as He pleased." That is to say, we do not need to convince or compel any individual or family to join our specific church. In fact, we should allow their decision to be purely driven by the Lord's leading. In Matthew 16:18 Jesus says, "I will build My church, and the gates of Hades shall not prevail against it." In other words, it is not us who build and, for that reason, we can rest. It is simply the Christian's duty to be faithful to the Scriptures, hospitable to every guest, and be prepared to offer answers to any practical questions visitors may ask. In terms of the visitation process for the specific possibility of joining the church, the following steps, which are strictly suggestive, has proven fruitful for our network churches:

1. The most organic first step is to invite the individual or family over for dinner as a way of personal introduction (this typically occurs naturally). During your time, ask to hear their Christian testimony, find out if they have been baptized, inquire why they are searching for a new local church, discuss their view and posture toward the Bible, and see if they have any questions about your specific gathering.

2. As an instrument to present definitions and clear expectations, consider giving the individual or family a copy of this document. We have found that guests are generally grateful to have a place to answer their deeper theological questions. Consider asking them to review the content and bring any questions or concerns to a follow-up dinner, coffee, or meet-up.

3. After the individual or family has had their questions answered and if they have determined they can unify with the doctrines, convictions, and liturgy held by your church, extend an invitation to attend the Sunday assembly and any fellowship gatherings for the next several weeks (4-6 weeks is typical in our experience).

4. After this time of visitation, prayer, and engagement with the other church members, request the individual or family to make a public announcement regarding their decision to either join or move on to another church.

In closing, making a commitment to a local church is no small decision. We, as church members, are to come alongside visitors in prayer, hospitality, and biblical counsel to assist them in determining the Lord's placement in His Church.

Article 09. Multiplication
We believe that widespread multiplication always begins

with local devotion. That is to say, expansion of the local church is not built on strategy or salesmanship or striving. Multiplication is simply the result of persistent faithfulness—faithfulness in preaching God's Word, faithfulness in discipling God's people, and faithfulness in shepherding God's flock. It is from this place of internal spiritual investment which God has declared to open the fountain of outgrowth.

Nonetheless, this truth does not eliminate our call to pray and plan for growth. Men who show the marks of future shepherds, teachers, and servants should be intentionally discipled and theologically trained (2 Tim. 2:2; 2 Tim. 2:15). Families who feel called into local church ministry should be prayed over, strengthened in doctrine, and prepared for the realities of ministry.

But as one might expect, multiplication (as a functional reality) is generally driven by church size. Now, there is no correct size for a local house church—the Bible does not offer us these specifics. However, biblical example, church history, and even modern science indicate that communities thrive when they are small. In our experience, the most fruitful churches typically include 8-12 families or 30-50 people (including children). Coincidentally, these numbers also align with the typical space available in the average house.

In addition to size, the central relational indicator for church multiplication is felt in the loss of the members' ability to maintain intimacy and fulfill the "one-another's" commanded in Scripture. This inability to connect deeply with each person (which is generally sensed by the body) is a spiritual signal that, in God's timing, this one gathering should multiply into two.

Multiplication, however, can be very difficult as it does place distance and spiritual transition between brothers and sisters who are very close. Nevertheless, we must remember that multiplication is God's work. Therefore, it is good. We, as the Church of God, are not to become stagnant reservoirs but flowing rivers on mission to saturate the culture with the Gospel of Jesus Christ.

Article 10. Planting

As stated in the previous article, numerical size, along with relational overstrain, are the physical the foreshadows of a new church plant. For those men who both meet the qualifications and are called into pastoral ministry, this opportunity will initiate the church planting process.

While Scripture is not specific on the exact approach for church planting, the Bible presents a variety of principles that have proven helpful. First, because the initial act of church planting requires shepherding, we are convicted that church planters must be gifted, qualified, anointed, recognized, and appointed elders (See *Doctrine Article 08 and Conviction Article 01*).

Second, both Scripture and history have shown that a plurality of individuals and a variety of personal qualities are essential to a fruitful church plant (1 Cor. 12:1-11; Ecc. 4:12). That is to say, in an ideal situation, we believe a church plant should include 4-5 families who are both stable in doctrinal truth and seasoned in biblical culture. As stated above, plurality without variety is often limiting. For this reason, we believe it's also useful to send off a diversified group of individuals who vary in age, maturity, stage of life, and personality type. While this is not always possible, we believe this multiform effort offers the most fertile soil for fruitful and safe church establishment.

Finally, we cannot overlook the strenuous and weighty spiritual work of church planting. In the weeks prior to multiplication and send off, church members should be in persistent and continual prayer for the new church plant. Furthermore, elders should be intentional in preparing church planters and off-going elders for the theological and practical duties of pastoral ministry. But most of all, the church must view this new plant as an independently governed but deeply bonded and unified sister church of Jesus Christ (Romans 15:26; 1 Cor. 16:1; Col. 4:7-8; Phil 4:10-23). More specifically, church members are to continue to commit themselves to prayer and make themselves available to the individuals and families of the new church plant while it takes root.

Church planting is true missional work. It is the central way of expanding the Kingdom of God on earth. It is an old Hebrew proverb that states, "Apples are not the central fruit of the tree. No… it is new apple trees." It is from this perspective and Commission of God that we labor. To Him, be the glory! Amen.

Section Five

FREE-WORSHIP LITURGY

• *Liber Adoro Sacrae Liturgiae* •

Introduction

Free-Worship Liturgy

"Let all things be done decently and in order."
1 Corinthians 14:40

Liturgy is simply a term to describe the order of which
assembled church worship is conducted. In fact, every
local church has some form of liturgy. In the Western
evangelical church it may look something like this:

Modern Church Service

Welcome > Worship Songs > Prayer > Announcements >
Sermon > Altar Call > Offering > Prayer > Dismissal.

In the Presbyterian, Lutheran, or Anglican church, the
liturgy is far more robust, including repetitions of doctrinal
positions, call and response activities, Scripture readings,
communion, and benediction. Historically speaking,
the liturgical templates are endless. Unfortunately, most
liturgically focused churches have manufactured extra-
biblical, dense, and generally and soul-crushing liturgies.

Clergy or church overseers often overextend their theological aspirations for the flock and bury the biblical objective of edification under a mountain of lifeless activity. Furthermore, by elevating the liturgy beyond the biblical instruction, many churches have squeezed the Holy Spirit's leadership right out the assembly. That is, through a prioritized dedication to a ceremonial formality, they have replaced the organic leadership of the Spirit and the biblical order of worship with the predictable directorship of man.

Having said that, we do believe liturgies which correspond to the biblical order of worship and allow space for the directing and prompting of the Holy Spirit, the exercising of spiritual gifts within the body, and the mutual edification of the brethren are both fruitful and vital. We have titled this structure *free-worship liturgy* because it contrasts the highly planned, predictable, and often restrictive liturgies of the ritualistic-driven expressions of church.

Instead of rigorously planning each section of the church meeting, *free-worship liturgy*, while still adhering to an arranged and scheduled order of worship, allows space between each portion for free discussion and for congregants to respond, share, and contribute according to the prompting of the Holy Spirit within the pattern of Scripture.

We do acknowledge that not all liturgical elements such as welcome statements and church announcements can be found in Scripture. That is to say, we believe each house church is permitted to add operational elements to their liturgy based on their sociological, geographical, and circumstantial realities. Be that as it may, we also affirm that elders ought to be prudent and slow to add in any extra-biblical liturgical rites which are not directly commanded in Scripture.

Below, we have offered the Relearn.org general liturgy, which includes mealtime and fellowship for your observation and consideration. It has, in our experience, served as a fruitful order of which can be generally experienced in three-to-four hours (including a corporate meal and fellowship time). Our Sunday gathering template is available to download for free at Relearn.org/Liturgy.

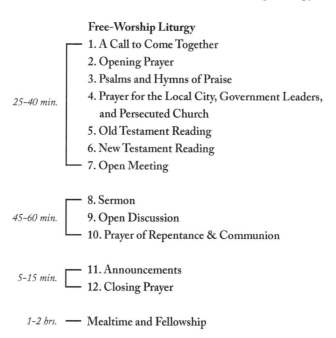

Free-Worship Liturgy

25-40 min.
1. A Call to Come Together
2. Opening Prayer
3. Psalms and Hymns of Praise
4. Prayer for the Local City, Government Leaders, and Persecuted Church
5. Old Testament Reading
6. New Testament Reading
7. Open Meeting

45-60 min.
8. Sermon
9. Open Discussion
10. Prayer of Repentance & Communion

5-15 min.
11. Announcements
12. Closing Prayer

1-2 hrs. — Mealtime and Fellowship

Free-Worship Liturgy

The Order of Biblical Worship

1. A Call to Come Together

(1 Cor. 14:26; Heb. 10:25; 1 Cor. 11:17–18)

Conducted generally by an elder or by the man of the home in which the church is gathered, a verbal call to transition from informal fellowship to the formal meeting shall occur. The call to come together is a declaration to the body that the structure and roles of our common Christian life are about to transition to the structure and roles of ecclesiastical life. While this may seem strange to some, this principle is seen everywhere in the human experience. For example, a work environment shifts our behavior from private life to professional life. At home, we may be the leader while at work we may not. At home, we can act as we wish; in the boardroom, we must act according to our job description. Likewise, these transitioning conditions of conduct apply equally to the church.

This individual should continue by welcoming the congregation, acknowledging any guests, offering housekeeping exhortations or directions (location of bathrooms or where a parent can take a crying child), and quieting the room in preparation for prayer.

2. Opening Prayer

(Acts 2:42; Mark 11:24; 1 Thes. 5:17; Eph. 6:18)

Conducted either by the man of the home in which the church is gathered or by any other elder-appointed man to fulfill this duty. Opening prayers have no boundaries, but a prayer of thankfulness, blessing, fruitfulness, and order in regards to the commenced meeting should be in view.

3. Psalms and Hymns of Praise

(1 Cor. 14:26; Eph. 5:19; Ps. 100:1–4)

In accordance with the doctrines set forth in *Doctrines Article 07*, a man appointed by the elder(s) of the church should lead the congregation in voice and/or by instrument in the singing of psalms or hymns of praise. Although a man is appointed to this duty of leadership, this shouldn't forbid spontaneous congregational suggestions for specific psalms, hymns, or spiritual songs.

Suggestion: We have found it fruitful but not mandatory for house churches to have both hymnals and three-ring binders that can house any modern song sheets not included within your church hymnal.

4. Prayer for the Local City, Government Leaders, and Persecuted Church

(1 Tim. 2:1-4, Heb. 13:3)

The Christian's ability to freely enjoy religious life is dependent upon the leaders of their land. The elder(s) are to select a man to lead the congregation in prayer for the local ministry, the governing leaders (locally and nationally), and those Christians who live in a state of persecution due to the lack of righteous leaders in their land.

5. Old Testament Reading

(1 Tim. 4:13; 2 Tim 4:2; Acts 2:42; 2 Tim. 3:14-17; Rom. 10:17)

Scripture reading has always been central to the local church. In fact, St. Justin Martyr's *First Apology* written in A.D. 155 states, "And on the day called Sunday, all who live in cities or in the country gather together to one place, and the memoirs of the apostles or the writings of the prophets are read, as long as time permits…"[8] That said, Scripture reading without biblical context can be difficult to interpret properly. For that reason, we believe the elder(s) should select a man to not only read aloud one chapter of the Old Testament corpus but preface his reading with a brief (1-2 min) exposition of the chapter's context.

6. New Testament Reading

(1 Tim. 4:13; 2 Tim 4:2; Acts 2:42; 2 Tim. 3:14-17; Rom. 10:17)

Likewise, the elder(s) are to select a man to read aloud at minimum one chapter of the New Testament corpus with a brief (1-2 min) exposition of the chapter's context.

7. Open Meeting

(1 Cor. 14:26-40; 1 Tim. 1-15)

In accordance with *Doctrines Article 06*, the elders should open up the meeting to members of the church for participation (prayer requests, praise reports, personal testimonies, spirit-led revelations, exhortations, short teachings, song requests, and spiritual discussion) consistent with Scripture for the purpose of edification. This is an organic time that may include sections of beautiful Spirit-led discussion and powerful prayer, but it may also include awkward silences and unsuited topics. It is the elder(s) role to shepherd the flock gently through this time without exhibiting a spirit of control.

8. Sermon

(1 Tim. 4:13; Jam. 3:1; 2 Tim. 3:16-17; 2 Tim. 4:2; Rom. 10:14-15; Rom. 1:15; 1 Cor. 1:18; Matt. 28:19-20; 2 Tim. 2:2; Col. 1:28-29; 1 Tim. 3:2; Gal. 6:6; Tit. 2:15; Acts 15:35)

Within the parameters of available time and in accordance with *Convictions Article 02-03*, the elder(s) first and potentially other men bestowed with the gift of teaching in support are to instruct and exhort the congregation in biblical doctrine through the preaching of God's Word.

Suggestion: We have found it fruitful but not

mandatory for house churches to purchase a basic lectern or pulpit. This allows the preacher to separate from his family and children and stand (with his Bible and notes) in a place where all can easily see him and hear the content being shared.

9. Open Discussion

(1 Cor. 14:29-32; James 3:1)

In response to the sermon, the elder(s) should leave space for the work of the Spirit in prompting orderly revelations and/or edifying comments or questions from within the body.

10. A Prayer of Repentance and Communion

(Acts 2:42; 1 Cor. 11:27-32; 17-32; Matt. 3:8; Matt. 26:26-29; 1 John 1:9)

In preparation for communion, an elder or deacon should pray for the congregation, thank God for the forgiveness of sin we have in Christ, and lead the congregation into a time of silent prayer (1-2 minutes) where each member can confess and repent of their sins to God.

In accordance with our *Statement on Communion*, the elder of deacons should instruct the men to arise and serve themselves and their families and wait to partake together at his instruction. The facilitator of communion is to take the elements in his hands, bring identification to the purpose of the elements in alignment with 1 Corinthians 11:17-32, thank God for both the bread and cup and instruct members to eat and drink collectively as families and jointly as a church. The elder(s) should consider offering an additional portion of time (approx 1-2 minutes) for members to reflect on the meaning of the ordinance prior to proceeding.

11. Announcements

The elder(s) are to offer all members of the congregation a chance to share any announcements pertinent to the church (mid-week meetings, needs, birthdays, etc.).

12. Closing Prayer

(Acts 2:42; Mark 11:24; 1 Thes. 5:17; Eph. 6:18)

Either an elder or a man from the congregation is to close the formalized portion of the church gathering and thank God for the upcoming provisions of food and drink through prayer.

Mealtime and Fellowship

(Acts 2:42; Acts 2:46; Acts 20:7; 1 Cor. 10:31; Heb. 10:24-25)

Those familiar with the processes and consumer culture of the Western Church may be prone to divide the formal assembly from the informal assembly. That is, some may believe that the informal mealtime and fellowship are not part of the church liturgy. That is not true. In fact, Acts 2:42 states that Christians, "... continued steadfastly in the apostles' doctrine and fellowship, in the breaking of bread, and in prayers." We believe that experiencing fellowship through food offers a place of not only relational depth but also an opportunity for members to follow up with the needs, lessons, and ideas expressed during the formal assembly.

> **Suggestion:** In an effort to diversify the burden of cooking and cleaning, consider ordering your mealtime around an organized potluck. Additionally, we have found it fruitful to remind the congregation to each do their part in serving to restore the host home to a state of cleanliness before leaving.

Conclusion

There are a latitude of church liturgies out there. However, we are to view them simply as a tool for local shepherds to build up the church in proper doctrine and theology. All church liturgies should be both edifying to the church and rooted in Scripture. While it may seem smart to add additional, extra-biblical elements to your church's liturgy, we must be sure to determine if it is right to do so. As we mentioned earlier in this document, God's intentionality and precise specifications for the building of His houses of worship declare His expectation to hold to His orders. May we never make His meeting our meeting. Amen.

Closing

For more information and resources about planting or strengthening a biblical house church, please visit Relearn.org or our church planting school at StJustins. org. This document can be purchased on our website. This is a living document developed and copyright 2020 by Relearn Church. Written by Dale Partridge. Edited by the Relearn.org Theological Advisory Board. Version 1.0.

Endnotes

1 MacArthur, John. "What We Teach." Doctrinal Statement , Grace Community Church, www.gracechurch.org/about/doctrinal-statement?. Salvation

2 MacArthur, John. "What We Teach." Doctrinal Statement , Grace Community Church, www.gracechurch.org/about/doctrinal-statement? The Church.

3 "The Baptist Confession of 1688. Section 11." The Creeds of the Evangelical Protestant Churches: with Translations, by Philip Schaff and David Hay Fleming, Hodder and Stoughton, 1878.

4 Piper, John. "Biblical Eldership." Desiring God, 16 Mar. 2020, www.desiringgod.org/messages/biblical-eldership-session-1.

5 John MacArthur, The Master's Plan for the Church (Chicago: Moody Press, 1991)

6 https://www.irs.gov/businesses/small-businesses-self-employed/frequently-asked-questions-on-gift-taxes#2

7 "Danvers Statement." CBMW, Dec. 1987, cbmw.org/about/danvers-statement/. Danvers, Massachusetts.

8 Richardson, Cyril C. "Justin Martyr's First Apology." The First Apology of Justin, the Martyr, biblehub.com/library/richardson/early_christian_fathers/the_first_apology_of_justin.htm. Article 67.